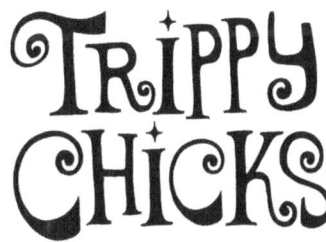 

Thank you so much for purchasing my coloring book!
I hope you like it.

Please share your coloring on social media and tag
@durianaddict.

COLORING TIPS
- Use a blank sheet of paper behind
each page to prevent bleeding
- There are some blank pages at the end of the book
  - you can use them for testing colors
- Don't be restricted by the linework
  - use it as a guide and add your own touch
by adding line weight and more elements
to the background etc - **BE CREATIVE!**

If you were pleased with your purchase
please leave a review on Amazon.

For more coloring books,
notebooks and journals go to
amazon.com/author/durianaddict

All my coloring pages are also available
in digital format so you can print them at home
or use them for digital coloring.
You can find them at **durianaddict.com**
and while you're there remember to subscribe to my newsletter
for a free coloring page, updates and discounts.

Happy Coloring!

Copyright © 2017 by Durianaddict LLC

All rights reserved. No part of this publication may be reproduced, distributed, or transmitted in any form or by any means, including photocopying, recording, or other electronic or mechanical methods, without the prior written permission of the publisher.

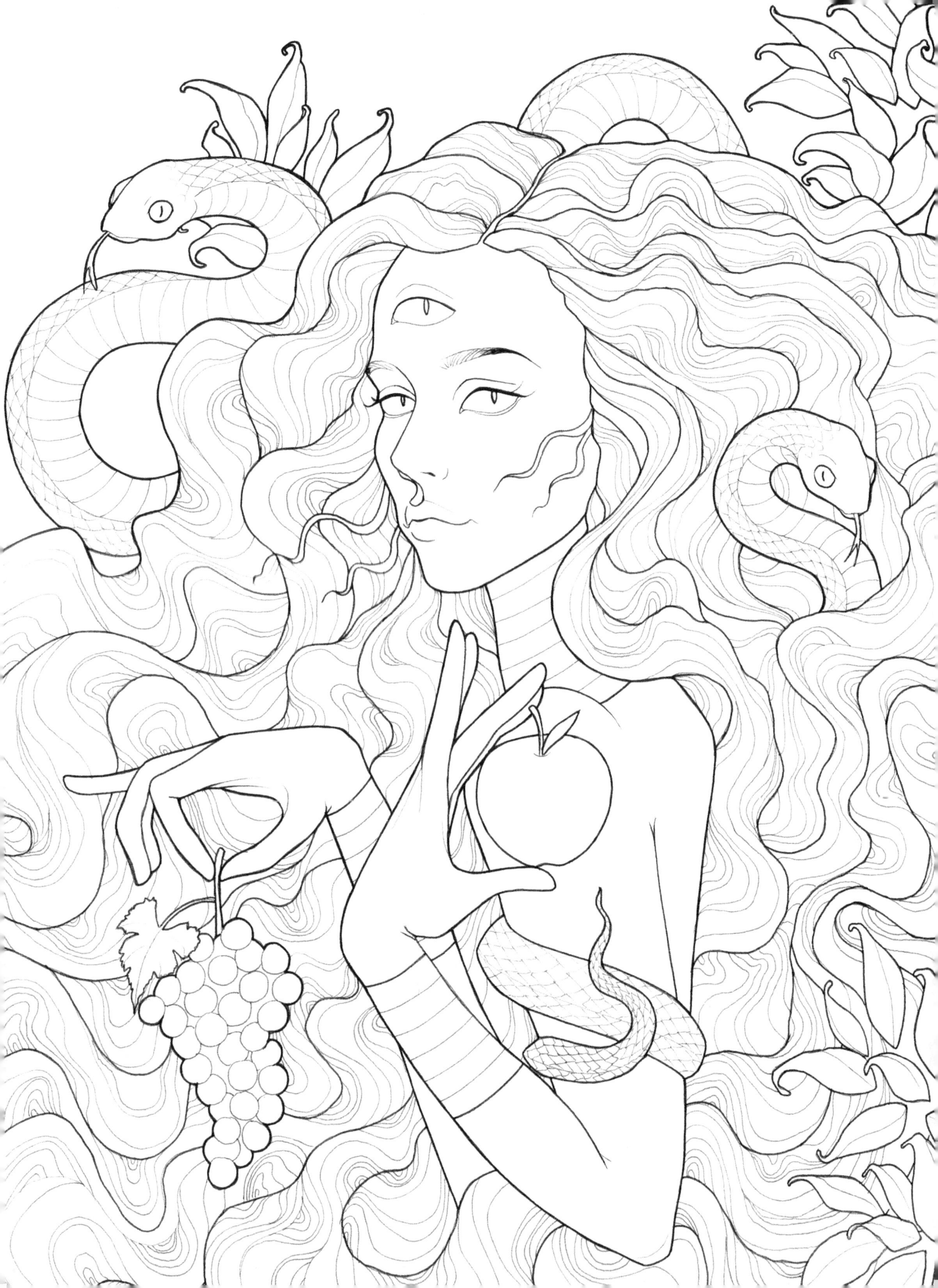

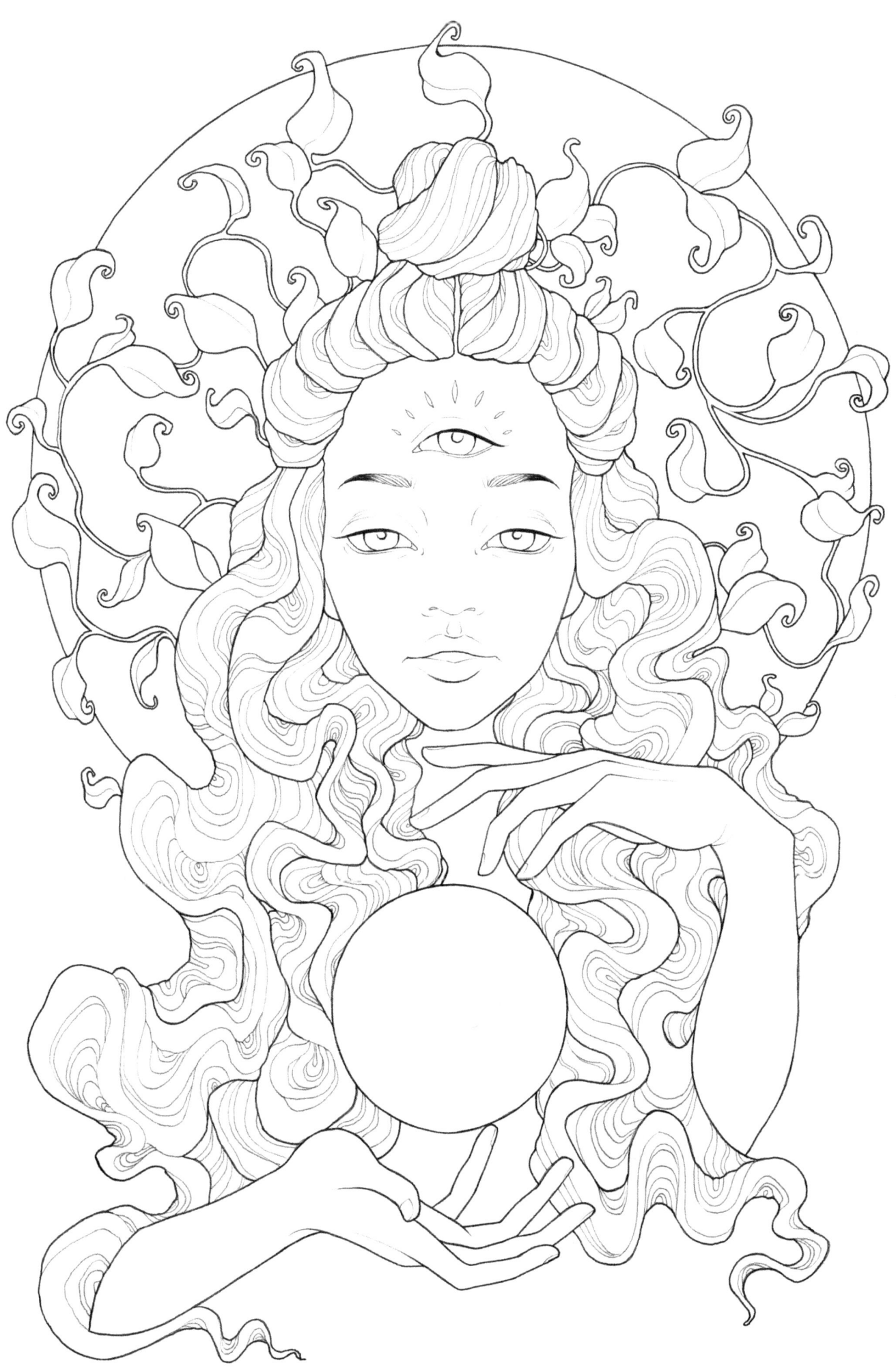

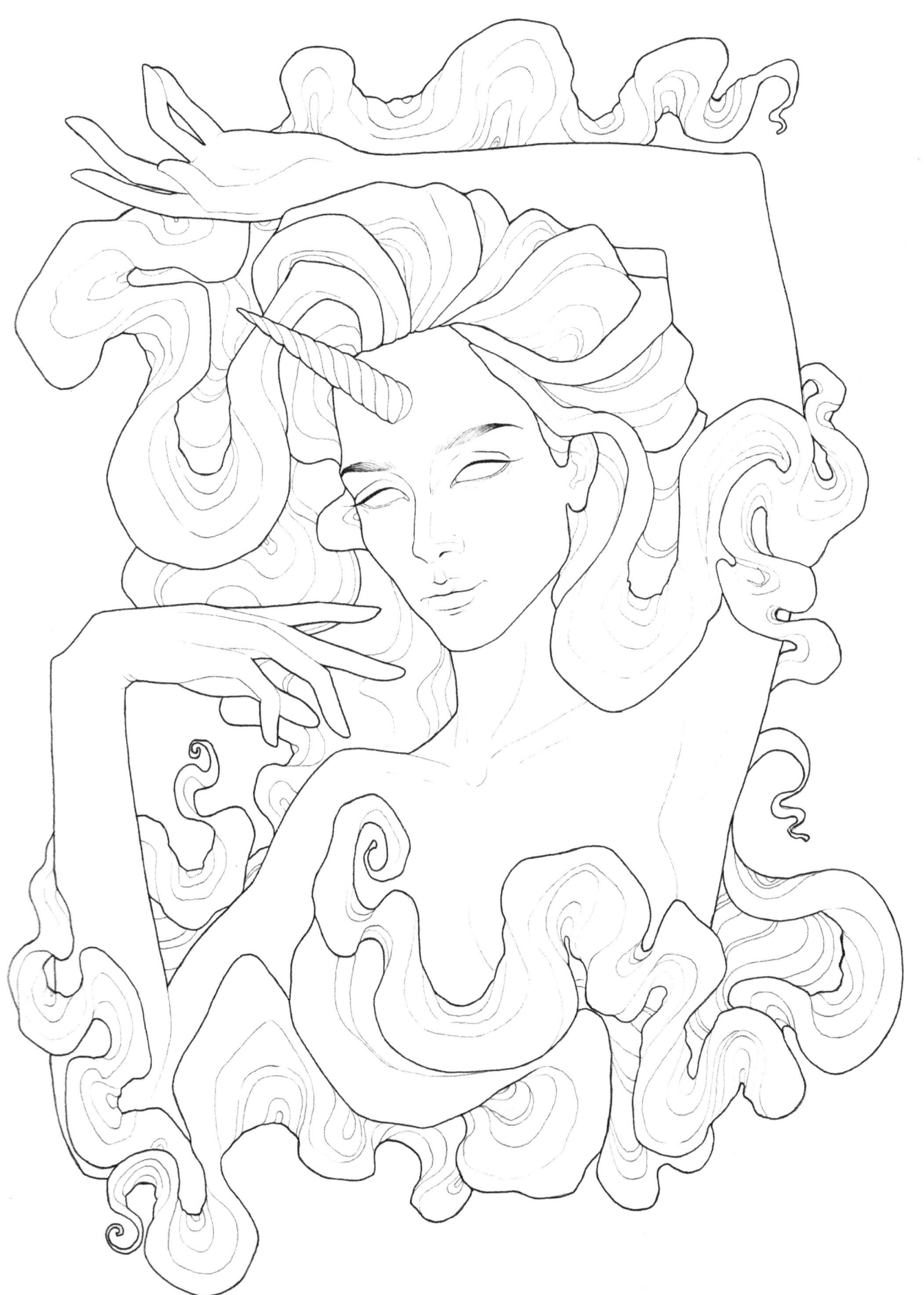

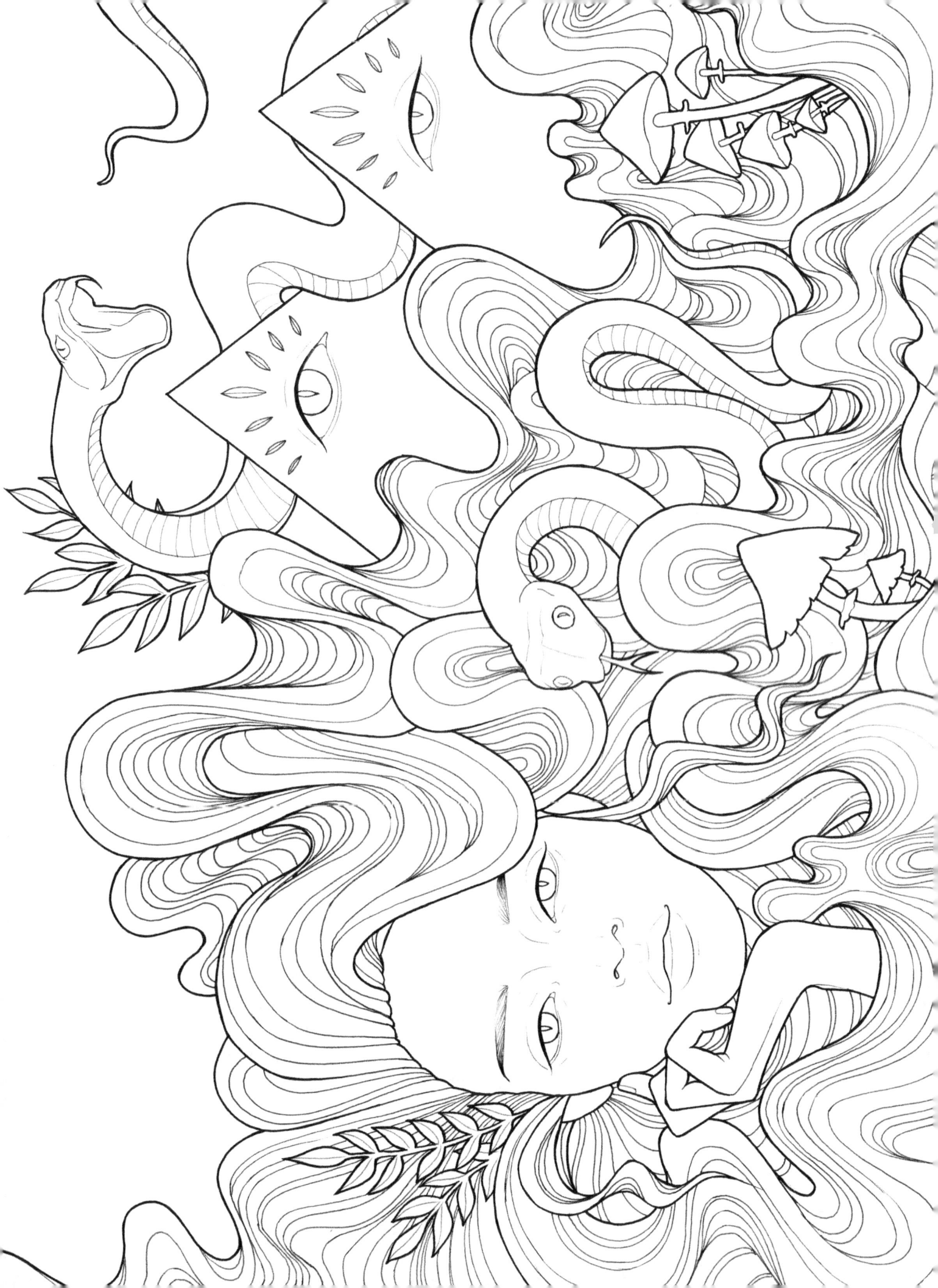

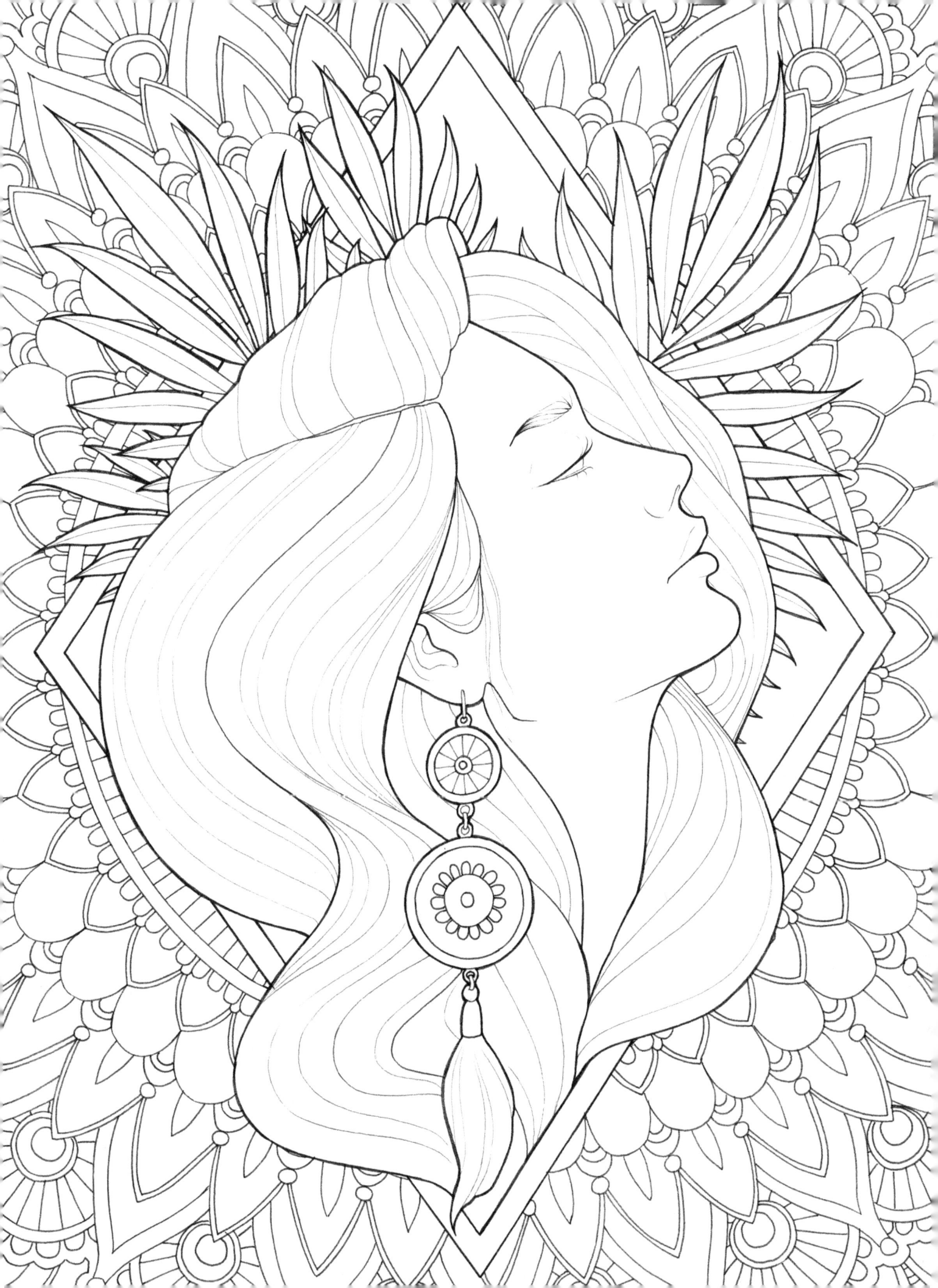

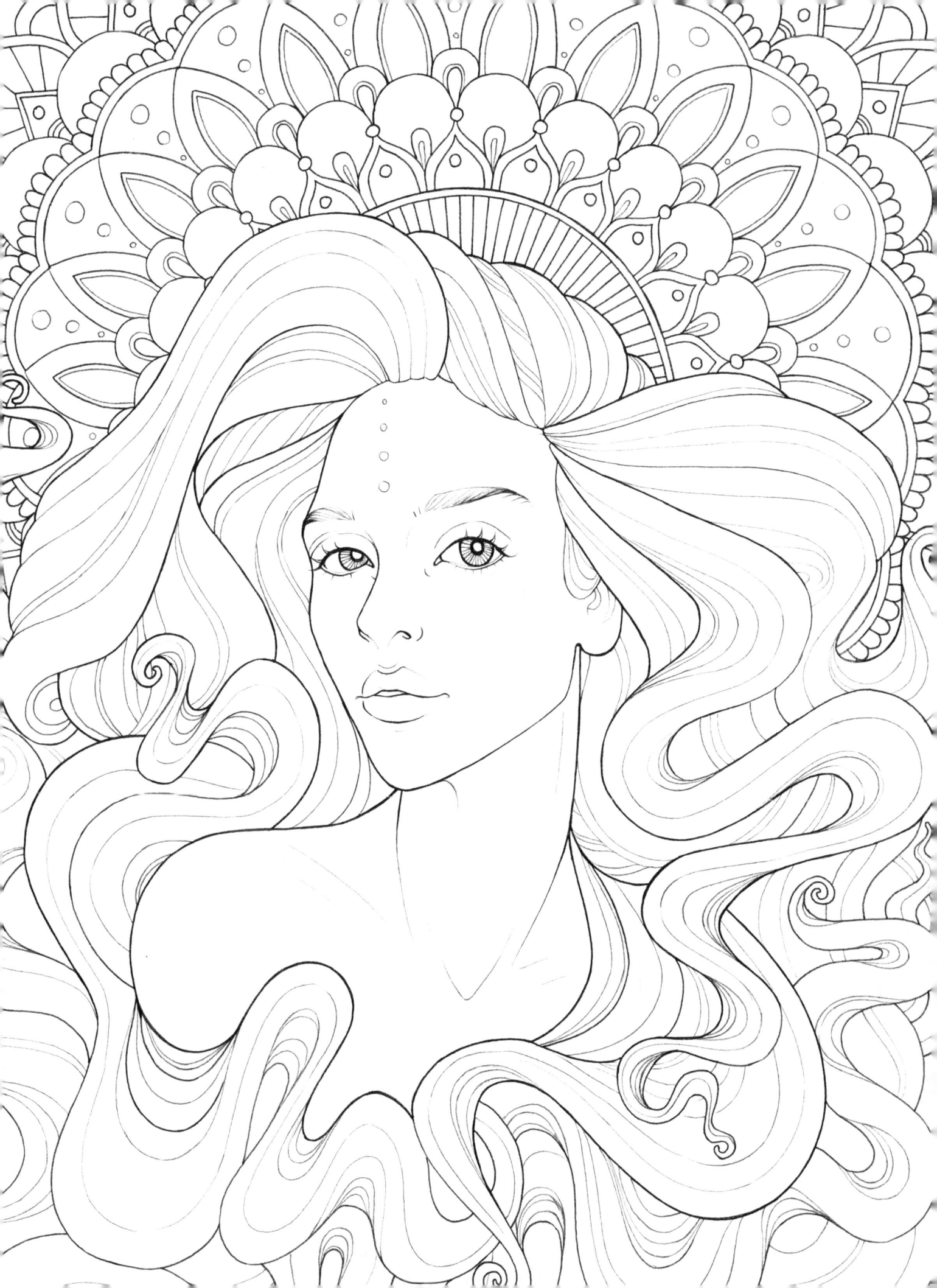

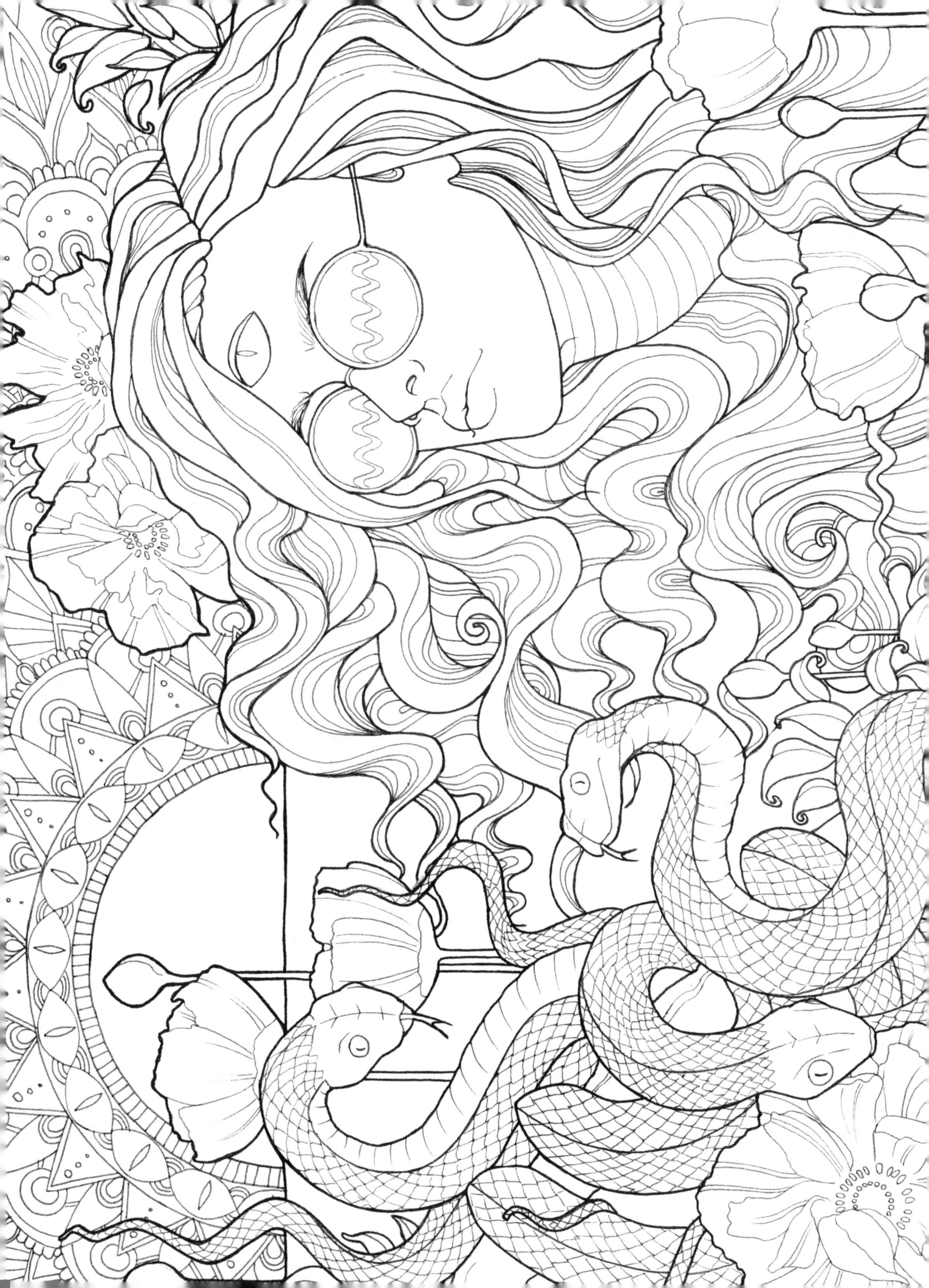

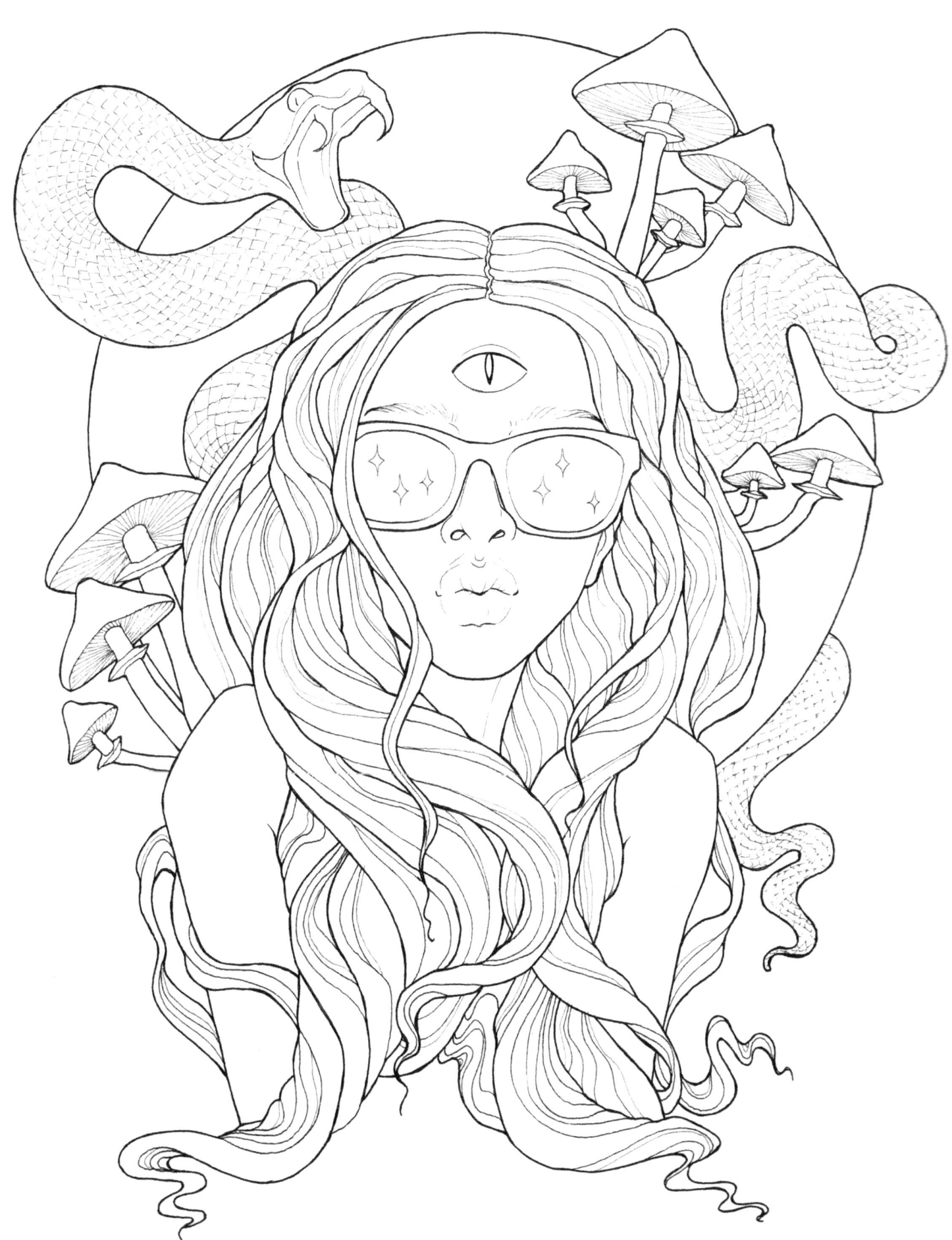

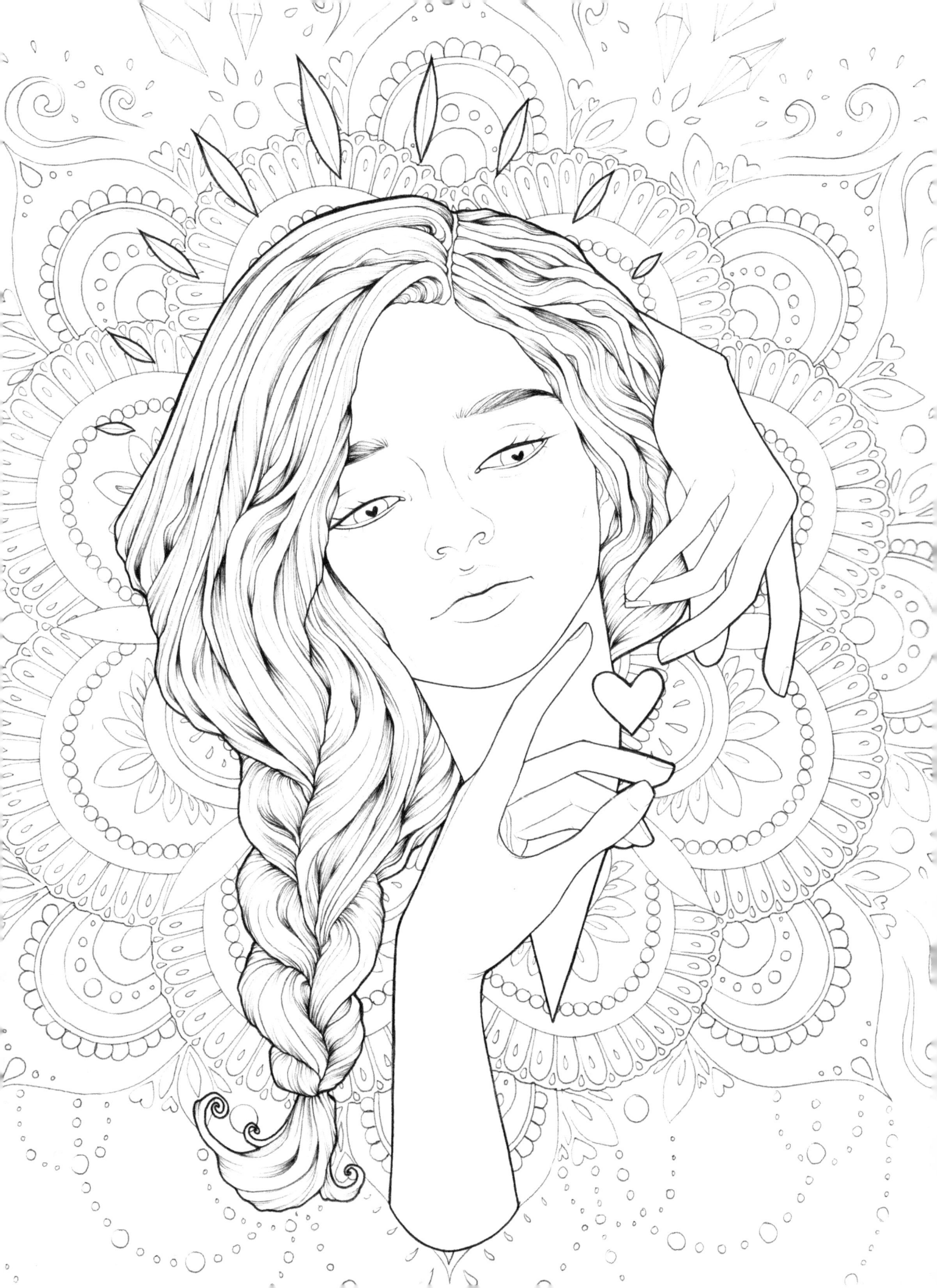

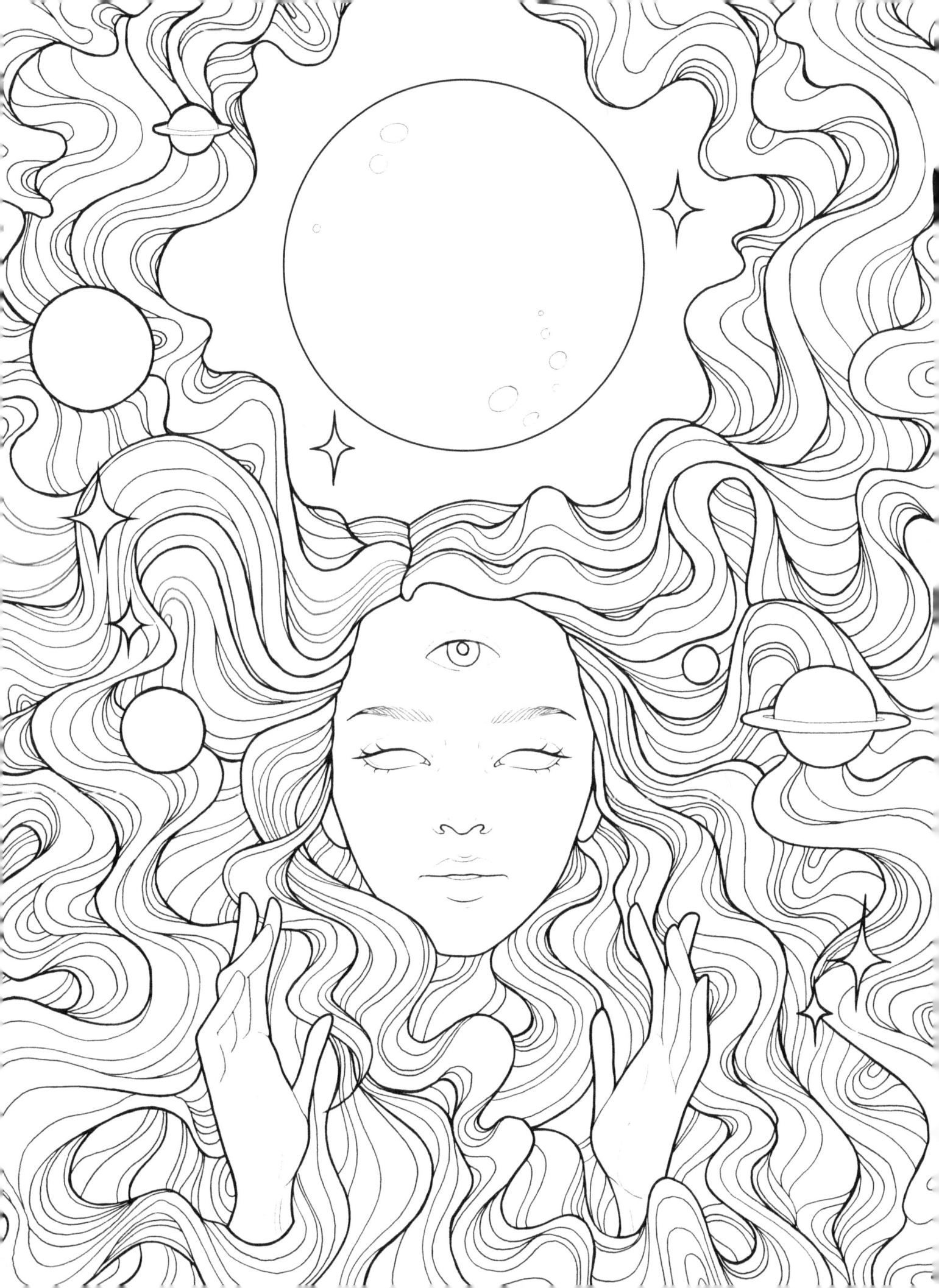

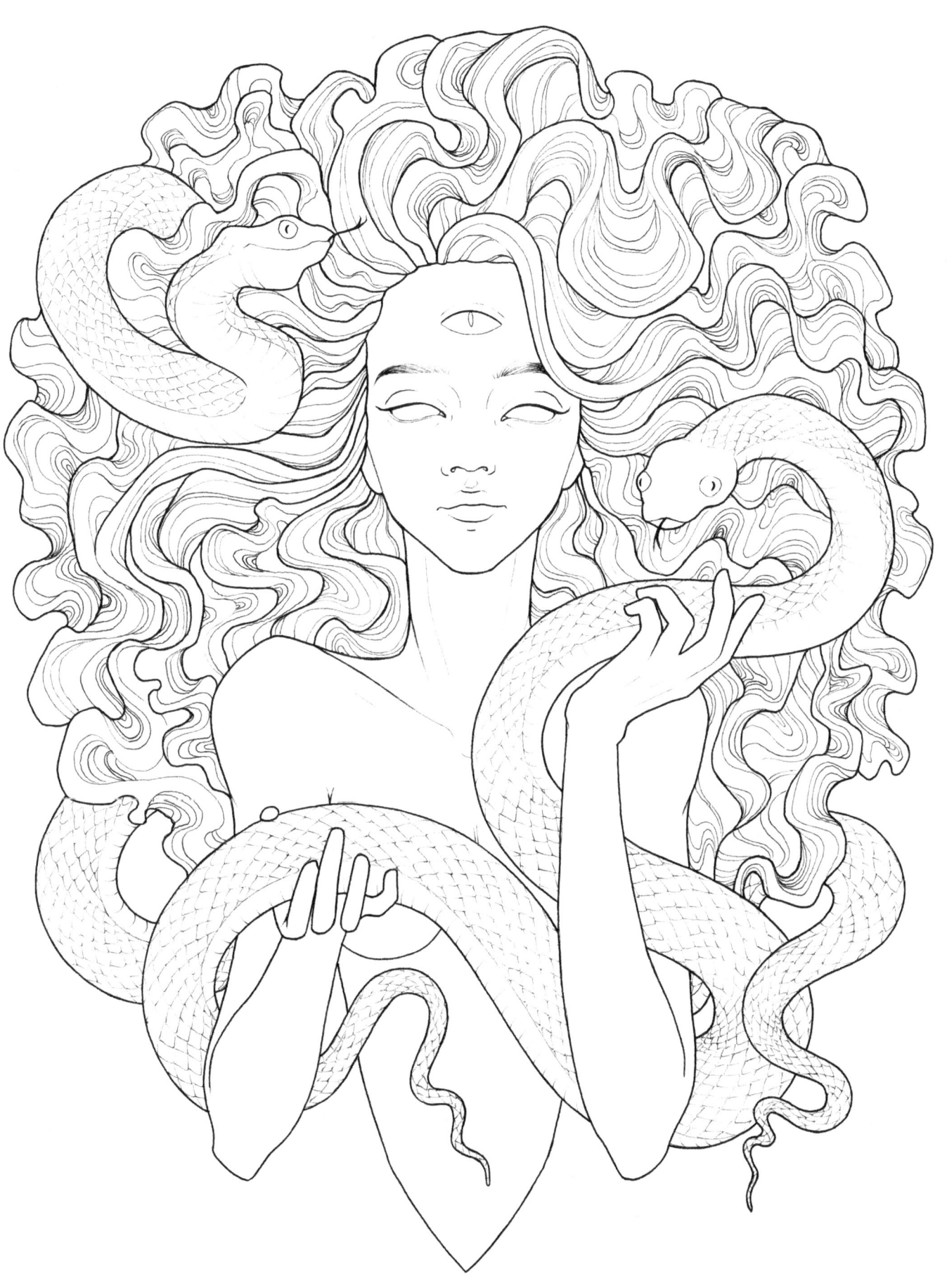

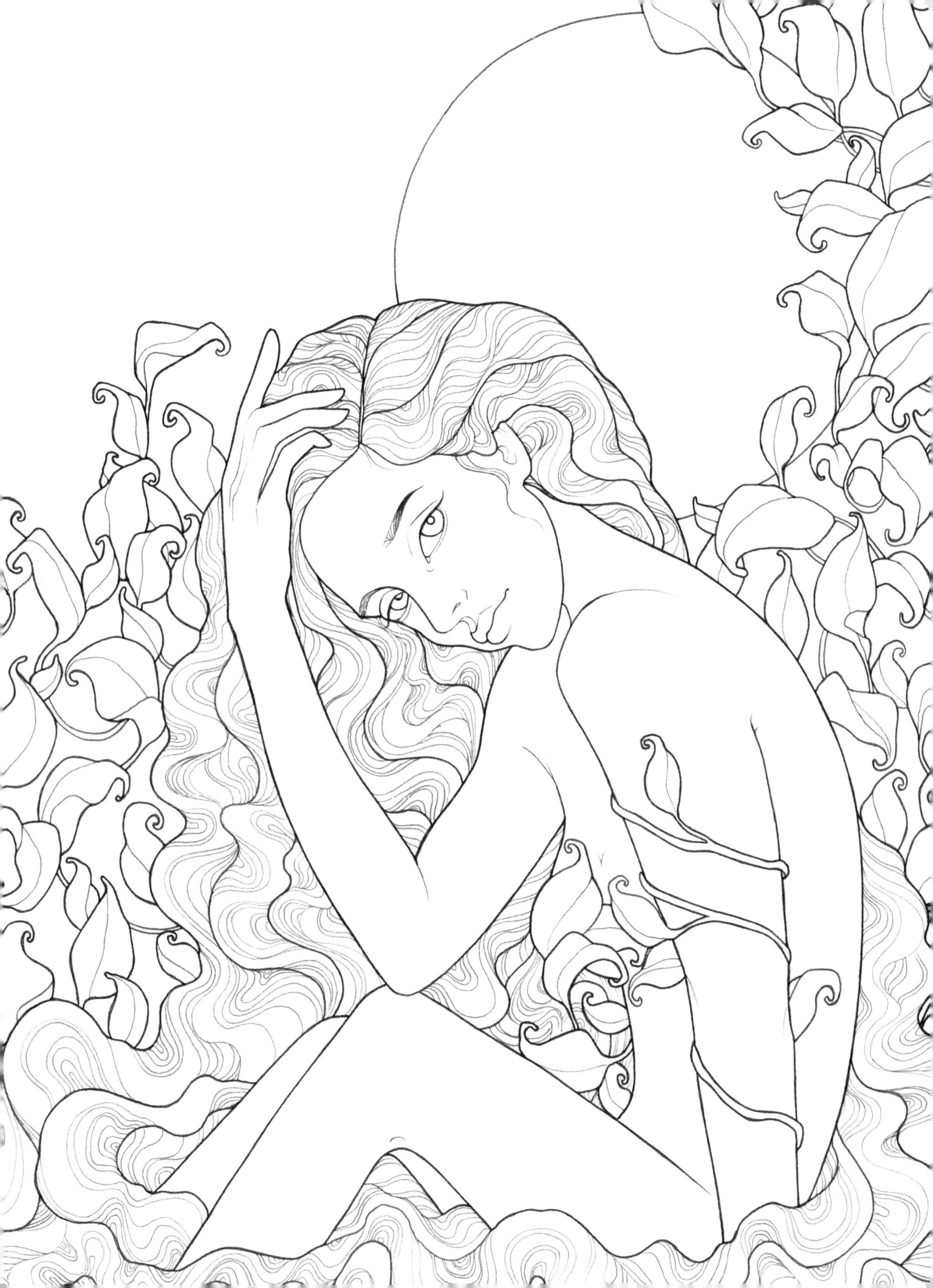

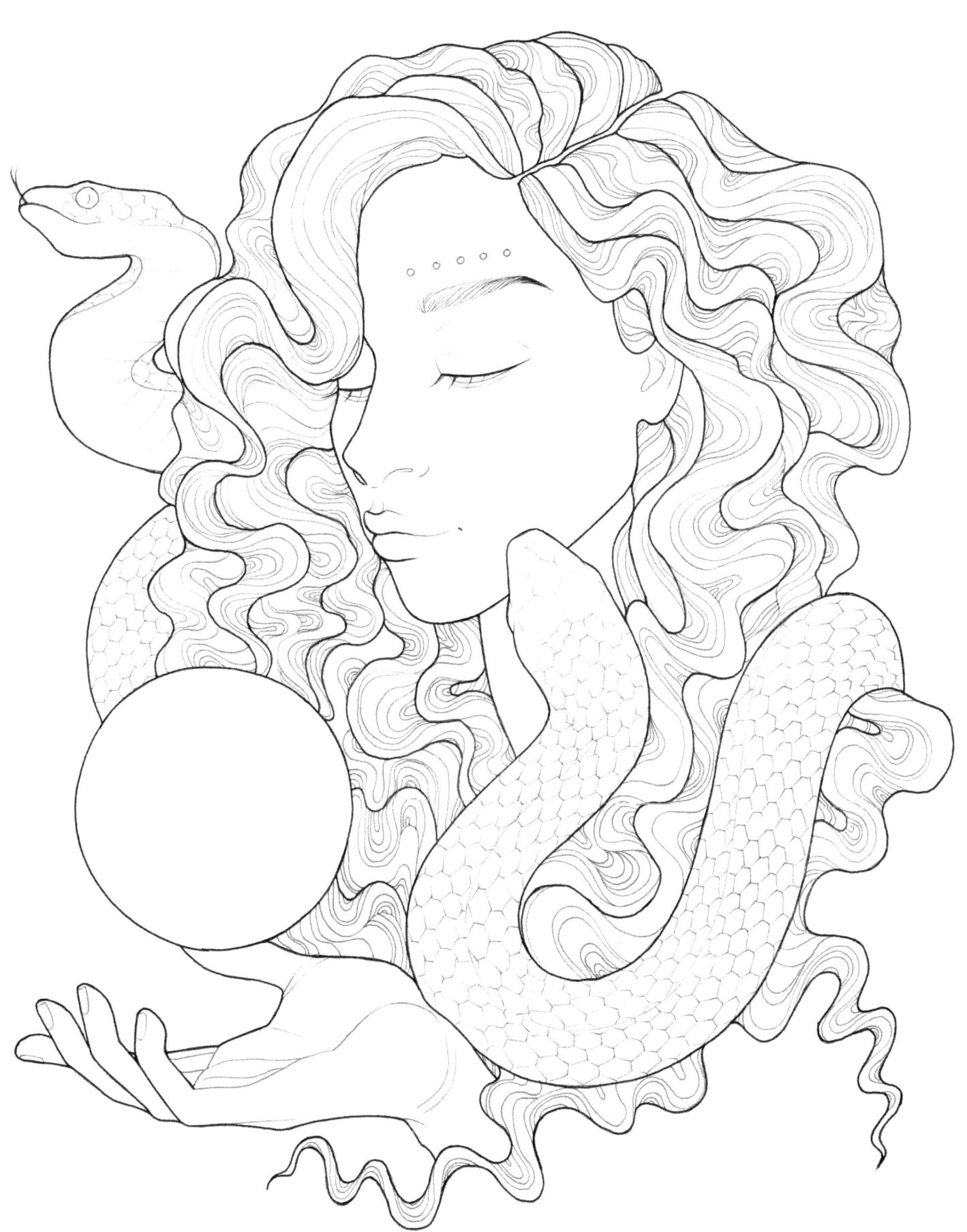

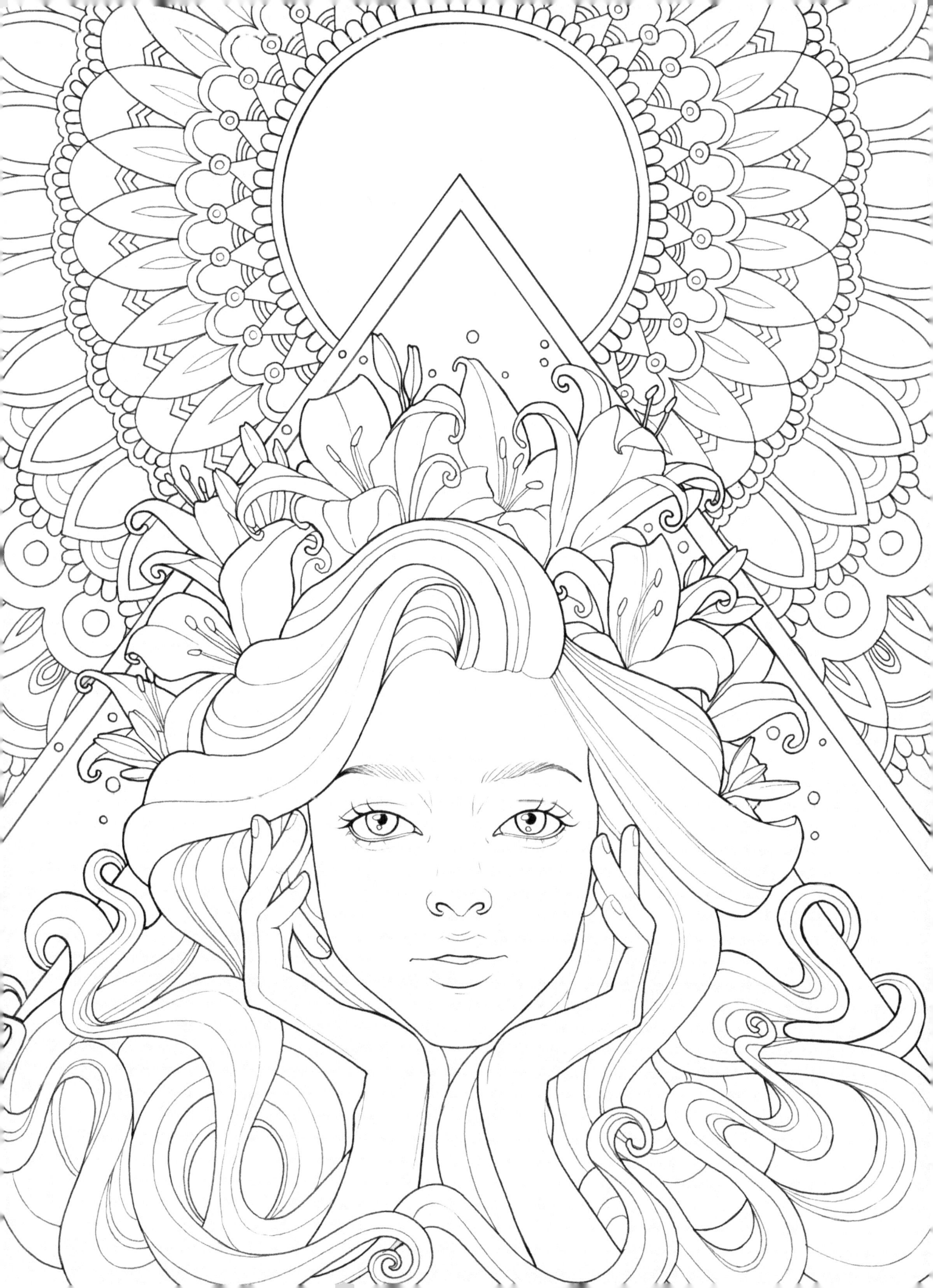

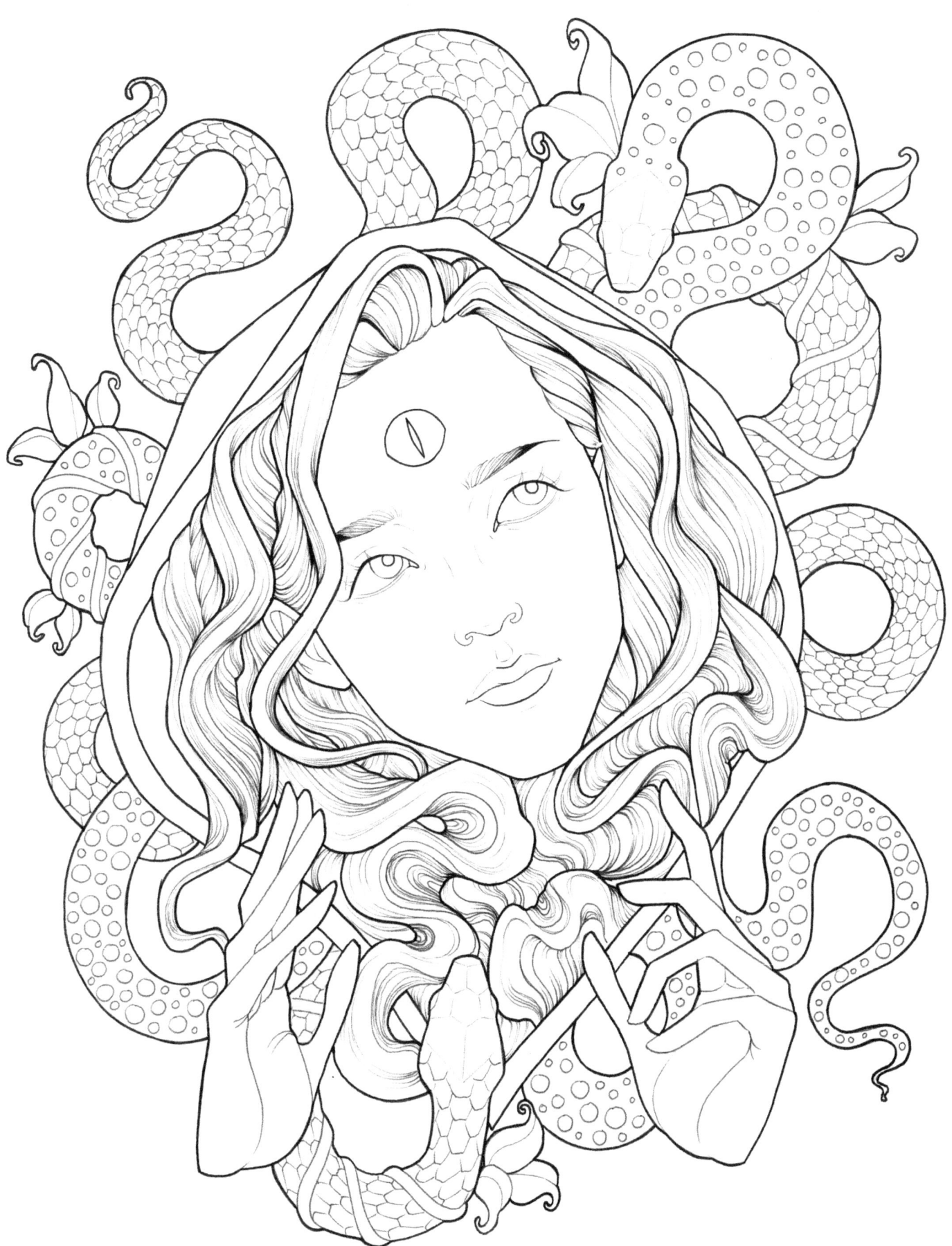

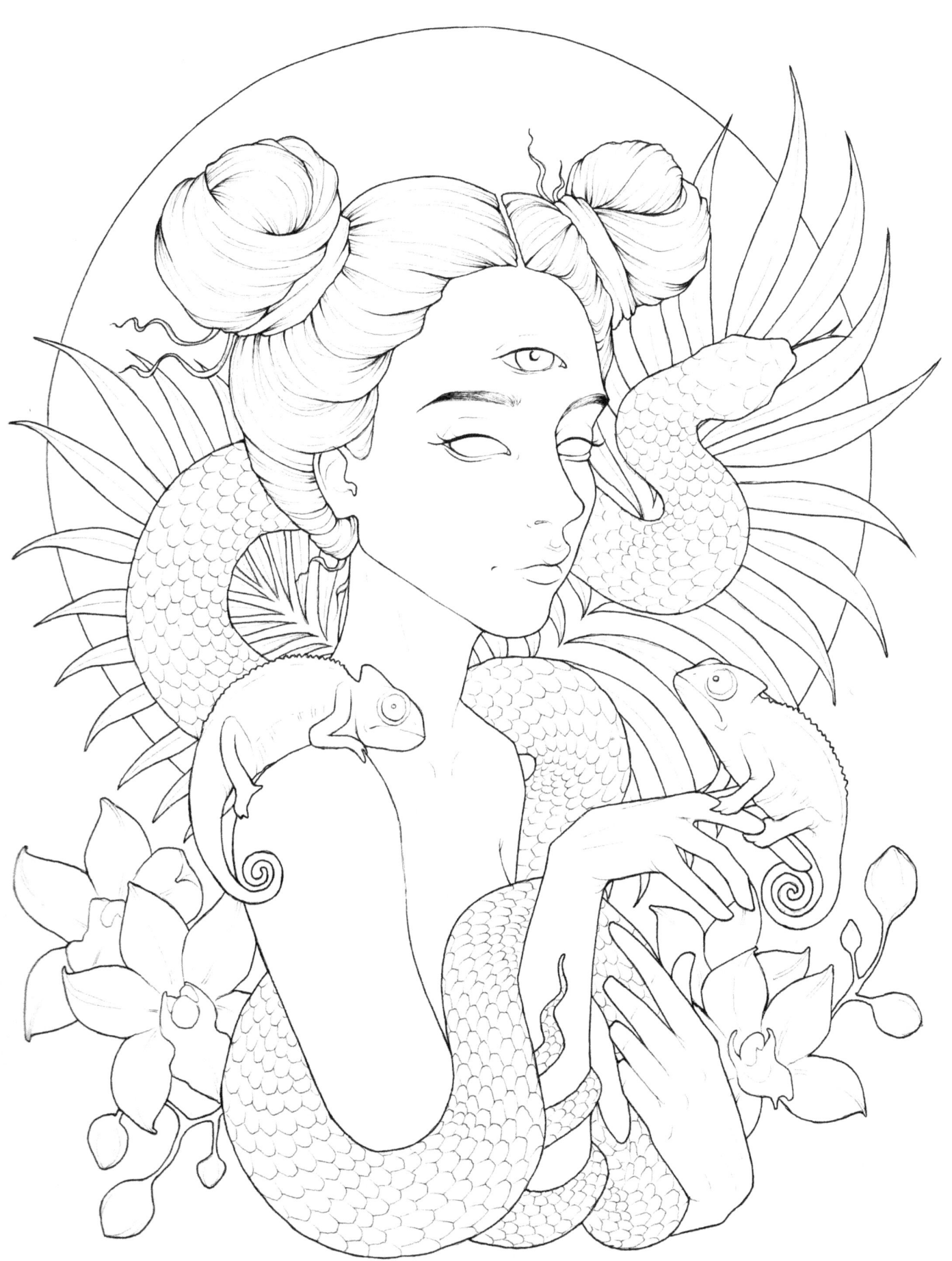

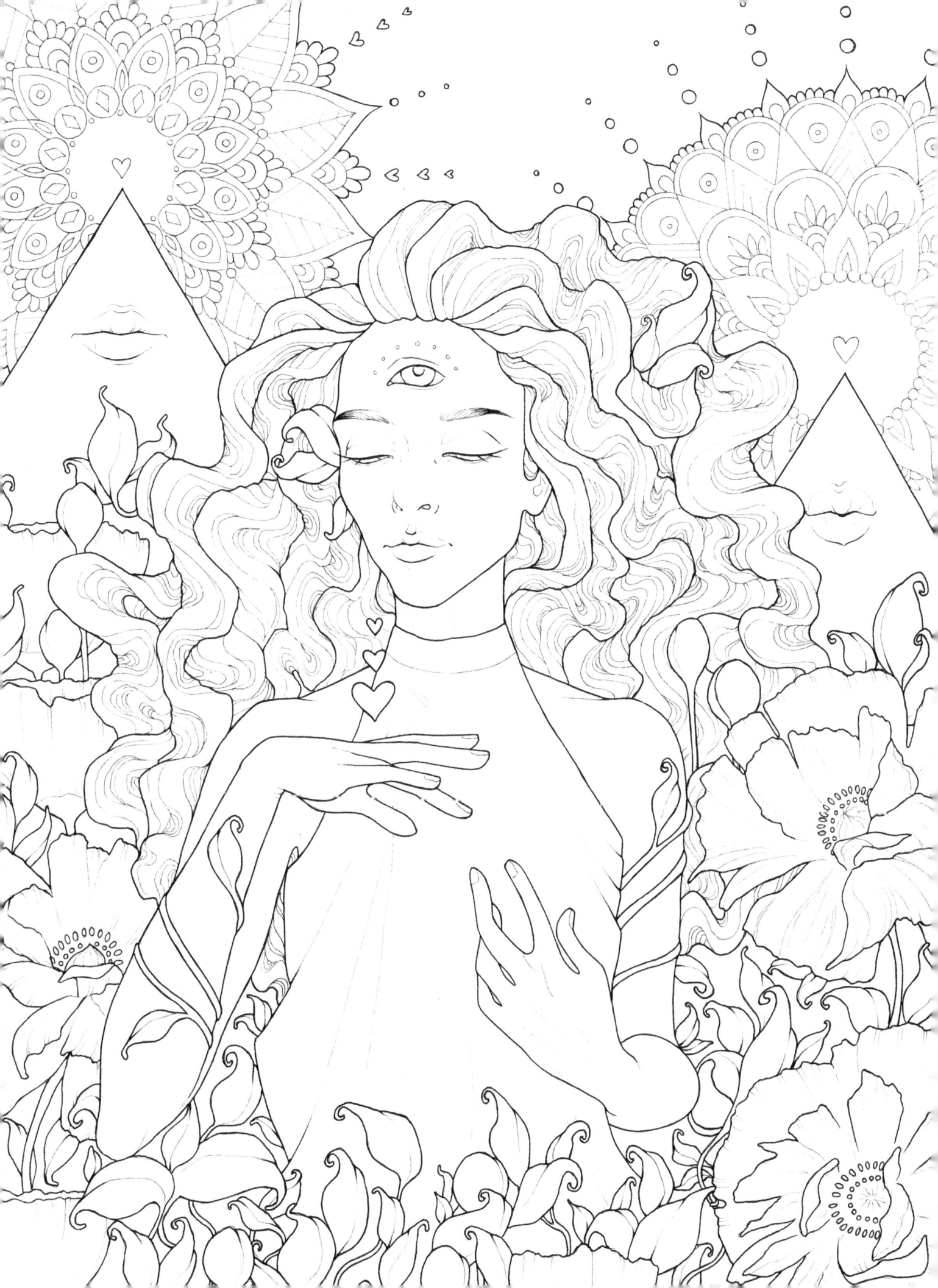